Edited by: James B. Patrick

Captions by: Elizabeth MacLean Laurent

Designed by: Donald G. Paulhus

Produced by: Fort Church Publishers, Inc.
Little Compton, R.I. 02837

Printed in Japan

Published and Distributed by: Stratford Hall Plantation
Stratford, Virginia 22558
804-493-8038

STRATFORD HALL
PLANTATION

Birthplace of Robert E. Lee

Photography by Richard Cheek

Introduction by Mary Tyler Cheek

Overleaf: Sunrise at Stratford's Landing on the Potomac River.

"flowing with sweete streams"

Standing high above the broad Potomac in Westmoreland County in Virginia, Stratford Hall has sheltered more distinguished Americans than any other house in our country. The first native born colonial governor, the only brothers to sign the Declaration of Independence, a brilliant general of the Revolution, authors, statesmen and diplomats all lived under its hospitable roof. They were the Lees of Virginia. The last of them to be born at Stratford was the greatest of them all, Robert Edward Lee, General-in-Chief of the Confederate Armies during the Civil War.

Stratford was built by Thomas Lee, an exceptionally able and vigorous man born in 1690, a member of the third generation of his family in the Colony of Virginia. Although the sons of most planters, including Thomas' brothers, were sent to England for their final schooling, he was educated at home, first by tutors and then at the fledgling College of William and Mary. He was an archetype of his time in history, responding with intellectual and physical energy to a new world of opportunity in all areas of life, social, political, material and spiritual.

Like most Englishmen Thomas knew that land was wealth; in 1716 he sailed to England to secure the purchase of a Virginia property that he had long admired called "The Clifts." The high bluffs that rise suddenly from the flat shoreline of the Potomac provide a sweeping view of the river, making it possible to identify at great distance ships sailing in from the coast. He was proud of his new acres, writing his brothers that they were "flowing with sweete streams."

Like his grandfather and father before him, Thomas served in the House of Burgesses and then as a member of His Majesty's Council. He also succeeded his father as naval officer of the Potomac and served in the lucrative position of agent for the Proprietary of the Northern Neck. Prudence in marriage was a high priority for ambitious 18th century gentlemen; Thomas' bride of 1722, Hannah Harrison Ludwell of Green Spring on the James, brought him wealth and property as well as shared love. Leasing his family's house at Machodoc, he and Hannah started the large family that eventually numbered eleven children, eight of whom lived to maturity.

Toward the end of the 1730's Thomas began to build his house on the "Clifts"; he called it Stratford after a family property in Shropshire, England. All that was needed for construction was at hand. Timbers were cut from the virgin forest; wide floor boards thirty feet long attest to the size of the trees that were felled on the site. Bricks were made from the soil underfoot; archaeologists have found the kilns in which they were burned. The thick walls were laid in Flemish bond, and the lower floor was given added visual strength by the use of glazed headers (brick ends placed so close to a hardwood fire that the silicon fuses with potash to form a glaze). To compensate for the absence of stone that in England would have been used to trim windows and doors, rubbed brick was employed to frame the openings and emphasize the quoins, providing a subtle change in color and texture that is pleasing to the eye. The balance and proportions of the H-shaped mansion and its dependencies, the sophisticated variety of brickwork and the elegant finish of the interior suggest that an experienced architect or master builder was the designer, but unfortunately his identity is unknown.

By the early 1740s the Lees were in residence. Eight children grew up in a setting that produced what John Adams later called "That band of brothers, intrepid and unchangeable, who, like the Greeks at Thermopylae, stood in the gap in defense of their country, from the first glimmering of the Revolution on the horizon, through all its rising light, to its perfect day." In a golden decade from 1740 to 1750 five of Thomas' six sons as well as his two daughters absorbed the ideas and ideals that made them patriots. Tutors – clergymen from Scotland – prepared the boys for their final education in England. Only the eldest, Philip Ludwell, was untouched by the new American spirit and remained loyal to the Crown.

The plantation on which the Lees grew up was a self-sufficient community. The principal crop was tobacco, America's gold, so valuable until mid-century that it was used as currency. Slaves tended the fields; more than a hundred lived in cabins scattered over the plantation. Indentured white servants from England provided technical skills, often training and supervising blacks. All food was raised on the rich soil of the cleared fields; orchards, vineyards and vegetable gardens surrounded the house; cattle and hogs were fed in the outlying fields. The Potomac provided an endless supply of oysters, crabs and fish.

The large landing complex must have been infinitely fascinating to the young Lees. Stratford was a tobacco port. Neighbors brought their huge hogsheads of tobacco to be graded and stored in the public warehouse near the dock and the assessor's house. Sometimes as many as thirty ships in a month anchored offshore to discharge cloth and hardware and books from England and to pick up tobacco and supplies for the homeward voyage. Thomas for several years engaged in the slave trade; the importation of human cargo must have aroused strong negative emotions in his children, for in their maturity they did everything in their power to abolish slavery.

Social life was important in colonial Virginia. Because of the distance between plantations, guests often stayed for weeks. In the "Northern Neck" between the Potomac and Rappahannock Rivers there was much exchange of visits, many dinners and balls; the Carters and Washingtons were neighbors and good friends. In summer there were dances on river barges hung with paper lanterns. Philip Vickers Fithian, tutor to the Carters of Nomini Hall, wrote in his famous diary that "Virginians will dance or die."

The conviviality of life in the colony was set against the strong realities of controlling the new country that was being wrested from its native population. Because Indians were continuing to threaten the white settlements, the royal governor appointed a delegation of Virginians to negotiate a treaty with the Six Nations of Iroquois in 1744. Selected as leader of the mission, Thomas set sail with his son Philip from Stratford's landing, bound for Annapolis, Maryland. Upon arrival, the group traveled overland to meet the Indian chiefs in Pennsylvania, where as spokesman Thomas negotiated the famous Lancaster Treaty which secured the loyalties of the Iroquois against the French and opened the settlement of the Ohio Valley for the English.

Thomas reached the peak of his career at the age of sixty when he was named Commander-in-Chief of Virginia to replace the ailing royal governor who retired to England. Grieving for his wife who had died a few months before, he conscientiously discharged the multiple responsibilities of his new position, but the labor was too much for his failing health. After only fourteen months in office, Thomas died at Stratford in November, 1750. His devotion to his wife was expressed in his will: ". . . if it be possible I desire that I may be buried between my late dearest wife and my honored mother and that the bricks on the side next my wife may be moved, and my coffin placed as near hers as possible, without moving it or disturbing the remains of my mother."

Following the custom of primogeniture, Thomas left Stratford and the bulk of his estate to his eldest son, Philip Ludwell, then twenty-three. His brothers Thomas, Richard Henry, Francis Lightfoot, William and Arthur, and their sisters, Hannah and Alice were left lesser amonts in descending order of age. The older sister Hannah had married before her father's death and moved to Peckatone, a large, neighboring plantation. The three oldest brothers remained at Stratford but the younger siblings gradually moved away.

In his will Thomas left instructions for his children's education:

"I desire and impower my ex'ors who I appoint Guardians to my children to educate my children in such manner as they think Fitt Religiously and virtuously and if necessary to bind them to any profession or Trade, soe that they may Learn to get their Living honestly."

Named as guardian of his brothers and sisters, Philip proved to be penurious and strict, so unpleasant and slow in giving them their small legacies that the youngest three appealed to the Court to have their cousin, Henry Lee, appointed their guardian, and the petition was granted.

Under Henry's pressure Philip saw to it that Arthur was sent to Eton, but he kept a tight rein on the young student, writing to the headmaster:

"I desire my brother may have a suit of plain cloaths . . . such as is fit for a boy of his age . . . one plain winter suit and one plain summer suit in a year . . . He will have little or no occasion for pocket money as he is to get his living by his head and has not an estate to support him as a gentleman without a profession, so the more he minds his studies the less time he will have to spend money."

Arthur applied himself as directed and went on to the University of Edinburgh to earn a degree in medicine, but soon discovered that his true avocation was in the world of politics and decided to read law in London instead. William, his next and closest brother, had remained at home but soon joined him in England. The two became deeply involved in the political scene; Arthur wrote a series of pamphlets criticizing Parliament and was named secret agent for the Continental Congress. William was elected Sheriff of London and later an alderman of the city, the only American ever to hold that office. The brothers could have had successful careers as Englishmen, but the powerful spirit of independence drew them rapidly into the American cause. Arthur was named Secret Agent by Congress and shortly thereafter both brothers were named Commissioners to France. Arthur was instrumental in negotiating the treaties of alliance and commerce with France, greatly strengthening the American Revolution.

Alice, too, escaped from Stratford to London.

There she met and married Dr. William Shippen of Philadelphia and returned with him to live in a house that still stands close to the Pennsylvania State House. Their hospitable home welcomed Alice's brothers and other Virginians and friends as they served in the Continental Congress. Dr. Shippen was an ardent patriot and later became Chief of the Medical Department of the Continental Army.

Meanwhile life at Stratford had changed radically for the better. In the late 1750's romance blossomed for three of the bachelors still at home. Thomas and Richard Henry married sisters, Mary and Anne Aylett; Philip Ludwell married his beautiful young ward, Elizabeth Steptoe. Elizabeth brought Stratford alive with her love of social life. She also wrought a miracle in the disposition of her husband, who softened his manner and became a doting father of their two daughters, Matilda and Flora. Nothing was too good for his girls; he imported the finest clothes and books for them from England; governesses, music, dancing and drawing masters instructed them in the gentler arts.

The plantation reached a peak of prosperity under Philip's management. Stratford Landing became an official port, several buildings were added to the landing complex, and in the stables, a thoroughbred stallion, Dotterel, imported from England, attracted the lucrative patronage of Virginia horse breeders. The affluent lifestyle was described by one of Philip's descendants, Charles Carter Lee, several generations later:

". . . when I was a boy, the chimneys of the house were the columns of two summer houses between which there was a balustrade, and in Col. Philip Lee's time, during the evening promenade of ladies and gentlemen, a band of music played the while in one of the summer houses. Col. Philip also kept a barge, in which the family enjoyed the music of his band upon the water."

Philip and his family did not share in the movement toward independence that was drawing his five brothers closer together as the years passed. In 1766 they organized an association against the Stamp Act. More than a hundred armed men, including four Stratford Lees and two cousins and four brothers of George Washington, signed the association's "Westmoreland Resolves," the first of the many boycotts of British goods.

Richard Henry Lee, with Thomas Jefferson and Patrick Henry, formed the intercolonial committee of correspondence. Richard Henry's house, Chantilly, on Stratford property, became the center for Virginia correspondence, disseminating the information on Parliament and King that poured in from Arthur and William in London. On June 7, 1776, their efforts were consummated; Richard Henry, one of Virginia's seven delegates to the Continental Congress, rose in the Pennsylvania State House in Philadelphia and proposed the resolution that gave birth to the new country:

"Resolved: That these United Colonies are, and of right ought to be, free and independent States, that they are absolved from all allegiance to the British Crown, and that all political connection between them and the State of Great Britain is, and ought to be, totally dissolved."

When the Declaration of Independence was completed in July, Richard Henry and Francis Lightfoot, also a delegate, were the only brothers to sign.

The Lees' cousin, Henry Lee of Leesylvania, became a hero of the Revolutionary War, serving as a commander of light cavalry and receiving a Congressional medal for outstanding performance. Affectionately known as "Light Horse Harry", he was a favorite of George Washington. When war ended, Harry came home to Virginia and in 1782 married his cousin, the "Divine Matilda," Philip Ludwell's daughter. Philip had died suddenly in 1775, and when his widow remarried, Matilda had inherited Stratford. The wedding in the great Hall was a joyful celebration, augmented by a present from General Washington of several pipes of his best Madeira.

Matilda, alas, was frail; the births of four children and the exhausting trips to New York while Henry served in the Continental Congress sapped her strength. She died at Stratford after only eight years of marriage, at the age of twenty-seven. Harry, broken-hearted, continued his political life and was elected to three successive one-year terms as Governor of Virginia. After his first year in office he decided to remarry. Anne Carter of Shirley, a great granddaughter of "King" Carter of Corotoman, became his new bride, and in 1795 he took her to Stratford.

Four years later Henry was elected once again to Congress and he and Anne went to Philadelphia. Their pleasure in the lively social life there was short-lived; Henry's hero and patron, George Washington, died in mid-December. Henry was chosen by Congress to give the memorial address and described Washington for posterity as "First in war, first in peace and first in the hearts of his countrymen."

The death of his beloved friend Washington closed the happiest chapter of Henry's life. Back at

Stratford, his financial situation worsened and the plantation fell into disrepair. In the depth of his poverty, on a cold winter's morning, January 19, 1807, Henry's wife Anne presented him with another child, his seventh, a healthy boy. She named him Robert Edward after her two favorite brothers. The last of the Lee men to be born on the plantation, he was to become the most famous of them all. When Robert was almost four the Lees moved to Alexandria, and Stratford became the property of Harry's oldest son. Young Henry Lee, after a few happy years, suffered a series of personal tragedies that forced him to sell Stratford in 1822, and it was lost to the Lees for all time.

None of the "band of brothers" who had grown up in the house when it was new and had labored to bring America to birth lived to see the 19th century; only Alice survived into the 1800s. But no Lee ever forgot Stratford. General Robert Edward Lee, lonely and at war, wrote to his wife Mary on Christmas Day, 1863. Their home, Arlington, had been confiscated, and Lee was thinking of Stratford.

"In the absence of a home, I wish I could purchase Stratford. That is the only other place I could go to, now accessible to us, that would inspire me with feelings of pleasure and local love. You and the girls could remain there in quiet.

"It is a poor place, but we would make enough cornbread and bacon for our support, and the girls could weave us clothes. I wonder if it is for sale, and how much."

Stratford was not for sale. It had been bought at auction for $11,000 in 1826 by Henry Storke of Westmoreland County. His widow, Elizabeth, lived there for more than fifty years, longer than any single member of the Lee family. At her death Stratford became the property of the Stuart family, relatives on her mother's side, and during the years the house and grounds yielded to the ravages of time.

A remarkable coincidence saved Stratford from irreversible decay. In 1928 in Greenwich, Connecticut, Mrs. May Field Lanier, daugher-in-law of the renowned southern poet, Sidney Lanier, discovered the manuscript of Lanier's address in Macon, Georgia, on General Lee's death. Mrs. Lanier was an active member of the William Alexander Chapter of the United Daughters of the Confederacy and was deeply moved as she read the concluding paragraph:

"Resolved: That we invite our countrymen to unite in some enduring testimonial to the stainless life and glorious services of our departed General, and that in the judgement of this meeting such monument would assume its best propriety in the form of a great hall of fame to be built by such voluntary contributions as shall be within the compass of the humblest citizen who loved him and who desires the grateful privilege of laying some tribute on his tomb."

The following morning, Mrs. Lanier received a letter from her friend, Ethel Armes, a scholar working on the restoration of Wakefield, George Washington's birthplace eight miles from Stratford. Miss Armes had been to Stratford and recognized its declining magnificence; "We must save it!" she wrote. "There," said Mrs. Lanier as she put down the letter, "is Sidney Lanier's monument!"

The story of Mrs. Lanier's battle to purchase and restore Stratford is a saga of perseverance in the face of every imaginable obstacle. Gathering a small group of equally determined ladies from several states, she borrowed $240,000 to buy the plantation. The Robert E. Lee Memorial Foundation (now Association) was formed as the managing corporation. A few months after the deed was signed, the stock market crash of October, 1929, shook all but the stoutest hearts. The ladies were not deterred; they redoubled efforts to raise money to pay off the mortgage. They engaged the foremost specialist in historic American architecture, Fiske Kimball, to restore the buildings, and in 1935 opened a debt-free Stratford to the public. The Garden Club of Virginia restored the gardens between 1930 and 1934 and continues to supervise their horticultural accuracy and maintenance. Now boxwood and flowers, meadows and woods again invite the visitor to stroll and admire the orderly beauty that Thomas Lee created almost three centuries ago.

Stratford is furnished with original American and English 18th century pieces. A spectacular gift of furniture and silver from Mrs. Caroline Ryan Foulke in 1976 has created an unusually fine collection of the decorative arts.

Like Mt. Vernon, Stratford is guided by a volunteer board of women representing every state in the Union. The Robert E. Lee Memorial Association operates one of the oldest continuing agricultural endeavors in America on its 1600 acres of forest and field. The Jessie Ball duPont Memorial Library, given in memory of Stratford's greatest benefactor, is a center for education and research in 18th century life. The Association is dedicated to the interpretation of those values and ideals that inspired Thomas Lee and "the band of brothers, intrepid and unchangeable" to lay the foundations of our democratic society.

Mary Tyler Cheek

Stratford's handsome brickwork delineates a structure conspicuously unlike any other early Virginia residence. The Lees chose to build their house in the shape of a capital 'H' with its most formal rooms on the upper level.

The Library provided a quiet space for the Lees
to study and reflect upon their collection of
imported books.

A sundial stands in the center of the East Garden surrounded by parterres of English boxwood.

Overleaf: The Great Hall, thirty feet square with fully panelled walls fourteen feet high, is one of the most spectacular rooms to survive from colonial Virginia. Here the Lees received and entertained, surrounded by their most elegant furnishings and family portraits.

The Nursery served as both bedroom and playroom for the youngest Lee children.

Candlelight enlivens the rich woods and polished brasses of case pieces in the Mother's Room and Nursery.

Stratford's east facade in spring.

The bedchamber called the Blue Room includes a Lee family cradle from nearby "Peckatone".

In the time of the Lees, a roof platform stretched sixty feet between the chimney clusters.

The Dining Room was the scene of elaborate meals served with silver and Chinese Export porcelain. The squirrel from the Lee family coat of arms was engraved on this English coaster when it was made around the time of the Revolution.

Hunting waterfowl was important because it provided both sport and food. Among the many species populating the Tidewater region, canvasback ducks were a favorite eating bird.

The Library Closet was the gentlemen's withdrawing room where the Lee men gathered to play cards and drink spirits.

Stratford's doorways are aligned for architectural symmetry and air circulation; one can look straight through the White Room and the School Room to the East Garden beyond. The "hit or miss" carpet on the floor is similar to the rag rugs that were made on plantation looms.

Overleaf: The vista north from the house to the Potomac.

Today serene, the Stratford Landing on the Potomac was once a busy area as ships with goods from England were unloaded and then refilled with colonial products for export. The distinctive chimney clusters provided the ideal spot for observing these ships and served as a landmark to guide ships' captains, merchants and farmers to the house where they conducted their business with the Lees in the Counting Room.

The Coach House is filled with horse-drawn vehicles and sets of harness of the types owned by the Lees. The Bremo coach was used by the Marquis de Lafayette during his visit to Virginia in 1824-1825.

Overleaf: Stratford's Great House was the center of a self-sufficient community where the multitude of tasks performed around the house and on the farm supported the Lees and their way of life.

Robert Edward Lee was born in the Mother's Room of Stratford's east wing on January 19, 1807 to Henry "Light Horse Harry" Lee and Ann Hill Carter Lee. Robert's crib still stands close to his mother's bed.

The Great House from the West Garden.

The Parlor, redecorated by the family in the Federal style of the late eighteenth century, was the scene of card playing, tea drinking and music making.

The stone Slave Quarters housed at least two families.

Among the numerous implements of the Kitchen are a copper still and a brass spit-jack – the one ensured properly distilled liquors and the other properly cooked meats.

The Laundry was the site of much soaking, scrubbing and ironing of clothes which could be hung to dry either outside in the Kitchen Yard or inside during damp weather.

Hidden from sight by a high brick wall, the Kitchen Yard was filled with smoke, smells and commotion as slaves bustled between Smokehouse, Well, Kitchen and Laundry.

Stratford's lawn is bordered by a ha-ha ditch with sunken wall
preventing animals from wandering in from the fields.

The Green Room, furnished as a guest chamber, displays
Chippendale furniture and late eighteenth century prints.

A holiday decoration made from
materials grown on the plantation and
accented with an imported pineapple.

Stratford radiant with the cheer of
Christmas candlelight.

Tobacco and corn were the source of agricultural wealth when Stratford was built.

The Southeast Dependency housed the Kitchen and Laundry with sleeping quarters above.

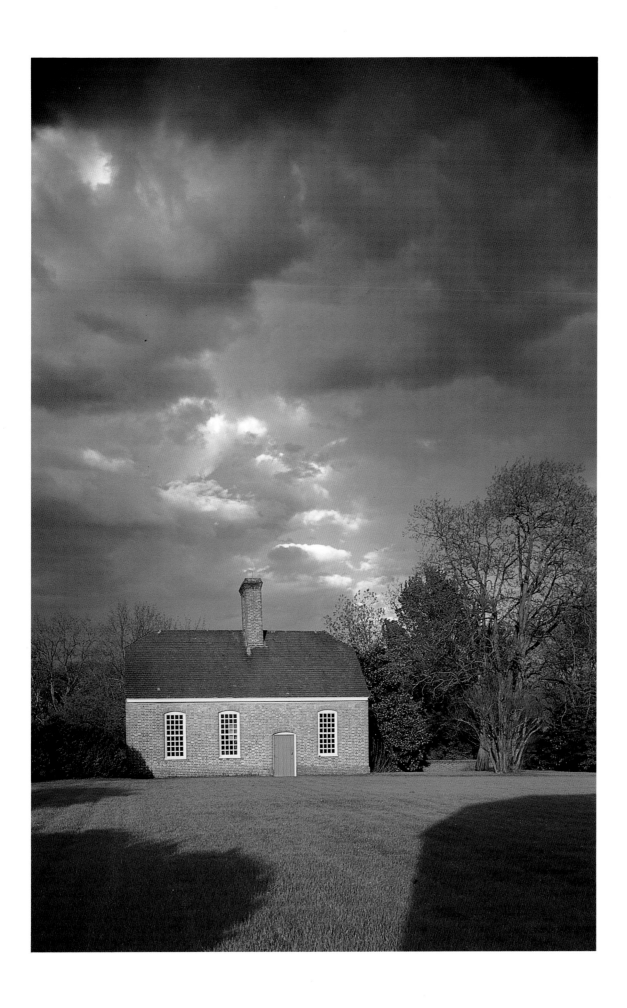

This hollow is all that remains of a colonial rolling road along which hogsheads of tobacco were trundled down to Stratford's Landing.

Exposed as the waters of the Ice Age receded, the Cliffs contain
visible geological layers filled with fossils.

The Kitchen was the scene of constant activity as indentured servants and slaves prepared food for the family and household staff. In order to cook the necessary quantities, several small fires had to be kept burning within the twelve foot wide fireplace.

Today Stratford's farm operation involves cultivation of over 300 acres, providing hay to feed the herd of black angus cattle and grains for the Grist Mill.

Stratford became famous as a stud farm when Philip Ludwell Lee imported 'Dotterel,' the second fastest race horse in England.

At the height of summer, the West Garden produced an abundance of flowers, fruits, vegetables and herbs.

Overleaf: The Mill Pond abloom with early summer's Mountain Laurel.

Lying below the Mill Pond, the reconstructed Grist Mill rests on original foundations and operates with eighteenth century wooden gears from a mill in Maryland. Neighboring farmers brought their grains to Stratford's mill to be ground into flour and meal.

HERE LIES BURIED
ELIZABETH MCCARTY STARKE
OWNER OF FIFTY YEARS
STRATFORD
FROM 1829 TO 1879

HERE ALSO LIES BURIED
RICHARD H. STUART, M.D.
OWNER OF FORTY-FIVE YEARS
STRATFORD
FROM 1879 TO 1924

A small cemetery of the Stuart family, relatives of the Lees and last private owners of Stratford, is a peaceful corner of the East Garden.

Glazed brick headers on the Southwest Dependency, Stable and Coach House catch the setting sun.

The Poplar Strip marks the original approach to the Lees' home.